I0117352

Theobald Smith

A ramble in rhyme in the county of Cranmer and Ridley

A Kentish garland

Theobald Smith

A ramble in rhyme in the county of Cranmer and Ridley
A Kentish garland

ISBN/EAN: 9783337132248

Printed in Europe, USA, Canada, Australia, Japan

Cover: Foto ©Thomas Meinert / pixelio.de

More available books at **www.hansebooks.com**

RECULVERS, FROM THE EAST SIDE.

A RAMBLE IN RHYME

IN THE

COUNTRY OF CRANMER AND RIDLEY.

𝔄 𝔎𝔢𝔫𝔱𝔦𝔰𝔥 𝔊𝔞𝔯𝔩𝔞𝔫𝔡.

BY

S.   THEOBALD   SMITH,

Curator of the Bridgewater Gallery.

ILLUSTRATED BY HAROLD OAKLEY,

From Sketches by the Author.

LONDON: CHAPMAN AND HALL,

LIMITED.

1889.

[*All rights reserved.*]

CHARLES DICKENS AND EVANS,
CRYSTAL PALACE PRESS.

TO

𝔗𝔥𝔢 𝔕𝔦𝔤𝔥𝔱 𝔥𝔬𝔫. 𝔏𝔬𝔯𝔡 𝔥𝔬𝔱𝔥𝔣𝔦𝔢𝔩𝔡,

Of Hothfield Place, Kent,

THIS VOLUME IS RESPECTFULLY INSCRIBED.

CONTENTS.

LIST OF PLATES.

PROLOGUE.

No classic strand or Eastern clime
Is here display'd in verse or rhyme;
A ramble o'er a homely shore,
That teems with ancient Saxon lore,
To roam o'er part of Kentish land
That welcom'd first our Christian band,
On fane's past glory but to dwell,
My subject is—no fancy's spell.

What ancient tempe or classic site,
With sculpture grand or columns hight,
Where pillar'd aisles or vaulted dome
Wrap saintly shrine or princely tomb,
Can to us more interest find,
Or both improve and soothe the mind
O'er land so favour'd still to roam
'Mid Cranmer's see and Ridley's home?

A RAMBLE IN RHYME

IN THE

COUNTRY OF CRANMER AND RIDLEY.

INTRODUCTION.

ST. AUGUSTINE LANDING.

Designed by the Author from an ancient Missal. Drawn by Harold Oakley.

WHEN first Augustine[1] fann'd religion's flame,
With holy band the saint to Britain came ;
Old Druids' rites and mysteries were driven
From wood's recess, and pagans' temples riven.
Whilst o'er the land the flame a radiance threw,
The saintly pile in glories rose to view,

Dower'd by the wealth and new religious zeal
Of Saxon Earls, and doughty knights in steel.
With Conqu'ror and his Norman warriors bold,
The cloister'd abbey Norman fane foretold.
Our later Kings their beauteous structures raise
To cherish'd saints, or some to Virgin's praise ;
And where the Gothic with the Norman vies,
Its sculptur'd tracery sending to the skies,
Adornment sacred in these early times,
For later fanes has deftly rul'd the lines.
In favour'd vales thus o'er the teeming land
The pious convent held its sister band ;
And holy abbots in sequester'd dell
With learnèd monks in sanctity there dwell.
Reform's stern hand then swept the nation o'er,
And future ages reap'd the fruits it bore.
E'en so the tranquil spot unknown to fame
Had oft in olden time a saintly name,
Where priestly learnèd of a former age
Have quaintly yet illumin'd o'er the page
Of vellum missal, where with pictures dress'd
Its early prayers are fervently express'd.
Thus o'er the valleys of this fertile land,
With golden corn-fields waving o'er the strand,

The old farmhouse once priesthood's home had been,

Where ivied porch and cloister'd walls are seen.

In halls 'gainst which the cart-wheel grimly leans,

May oft have worshipp'd England's Saxon Queens.

AN OLD FARM, KENT.

Where clust'ring hops now seek the shelter'd dell

Was heard the ringing of the matins bell.

On ancient times thus pond'ring as I stray,

In rambling mood from Herne's still bracing bay,

When shadows flit o'er all the downs so fast,

With thoughts I wander'd o'er the shadowy past.

Through fields of corn and barley's bearded stalk
And clover sweet, I, strolling onward, walk.
The graceful plumes of oats and tender rye
Bow homage to the zephyr's passing sigh.
Down shady lanes, 'twixt banks of wayside flowers,
Through hazy distance rise Reculvers' towers.

RECULVERS.

Where stands Reculvers'² church, from village torn
By ocean's ruthless power in frequent storm,
Whose ancient towers heard village bells oft rung,
In open aisles the tuneful psalm was sung ;
Its sacred altar free to ocean's blast,
Where moaning winds in gusts when rushing past
Oft stir the echoes of its bygone chants,
Sings solemn dirge amongst the sea-gulls' haunts,
For congregations long since pass'd away,
Whose graves the soil now loose has oped to-day ;
The crumbling cliff at Ocean's stormy call,
Slipp'd oft away with many a sudden fall,
Till churchyard reach'd the now insatiate deep,
Disturb'd the dead all in their long last sleep.
Royal Ethelbert, our primal Christian King,
Here held his court, where now the sea-mew's wing

Floats in the breeze, and oft the curlew's cry
Th' approaching storm now hails, on pinions high,
As wheeling round o'er the old gray worn towers
On prey intent withal, its light wing soars
Away to sea, where stood in Saxon days
The kingly palace, now beneath the waves
Which left no vestige of its stately past;
But saintly halo will for e'er be cast
O'er surge-beat site of this its kingly home,
Entomb'd in ocean, hid by lashing foam.
Through dim past days the ancient lore can dwell
On Bertha Queen, and chroniclers now tell
How one King's daughter from proud Gallia's court,
To welcome Augustine her people brought
(At Ebbs-fleet first, he touched the English land),
And to the mission lent her helping hand.
Oft in the Palace, now torn by ocean's powers,
Have Bertha's maidens pass'd their gloomy hours,
Those wild songs singing to the tuneful lyre
Of Norseman chieftain, whose fierce warlike fire
Was quench'd for ever by the heaving wave
That now flows o'er our kingly Saxon's grave.
Tradition now still marks where without trace
Sleeps this good King of noble Saxon race.

Reculvers, known o'er all this lonely shore.
"The Sisters," 'twixt the Goodwins and the Nore,
A landmark serves for ships when outward bound ;
These bearings show where treach'rous sands are found :
Now point the course—or where towards east or west,
And shrine for saintly King for e'er at rest,
O'er ancient Fort Rome's relic once of might,
And marshes' drear expanse unfolds to sight,
Where kine roam, and heron stalks so free,
And many a bird wind-borne from o'er the sea
Now sleep where bullrush rears its sombre head
'Mongst fenny dykes and plashy, oozy bed,
Which winding to the dim perspective far,
Finds Upstreet, Chislet, and the ham of Saar,
Near where the steam oft sends its whity whiff,
And Birchingtonia's bung'lows trim the cliff.

THE TREACHEROUS SANDS.

"A wreck, there's a wreck on the Goodwin Sand ! "
From mouth now to mouth it echoes the strand ;
The lifeboat's crew soon respond to the call,
Don their oilskins and life-belts one and all ;
The coxswain last takes his place in the boat,
" Now steady, my men—push off—we're afloat."

How winds whistle round, and how the waves roar,

And foam from the waves shuts the view from the shore !

    " O'er the foam and the spray,

      Where seas green and gray

      Rush and boil right away

      On sands night and day,

My boys, pull away ! now keep well together ;

We'll reach her safe yet, despite wind and weather."

They rise to the waves and pull fresh and strong,

The cresting sea-horses now gallop along ;

On, onward they go, and strongly they row

Above the loose rack, all foaming below,

Now deep in the valley, now high on the hill,

Through waves' ceaseless roar and winds whistling
    shrill.

A rocket now shoots far into the night.

Another ! another ! they welcome the sight.

    " O'er the foam and the spray,

      Where seas green and gray

      Rush and boil right away

      On sands night and day,

My boys, pull away ! now keep well together ;

We'll reach her safe yet, despite wind and weather."

Back wash the dark waves from the treach'rous sand,

The breakers soon show "the Goodwins" at hand.

Through scud as it flies, looming upward and dark,

Hull deep in the sand lay the wreck of the bark.

"We're sav'd! We're sav'd!" now sounds through the
    night.

"We're sav'd! We're sav'd! The lifeboat's in sight!

Her leeside well down!—Steady, boys, steady!

Jump when we tell you!—Ready, boys, ready?"

       "O'er the foam and the spray,

         Where seas green and gray

         Rush and boil right away

         On sands night and day,

My boys, pull away! Now row well together;

We've now sav'd them all, in spite of foul weather."

RECULVERS—*continued.*

Where angler now fond recreation plies

The finny tribe to lure, he peaceful tries

With taper rod and line of finest make,

To fill his basket with his scaly take,

Great Cæsar's galleys snug at anchor lay

From morn to eve—which mark'd the close of day—

His legions landing at Regulbium's fort
From sailing from the old Rutupium's port,
For here had ebb'd a stream with tidal wave,
Which thus the name of island Thanet gave.

RECULVERS.

As Wantsume erst was then the channel known,[3]
'Mid old Reculver and quaint Richboro' town,
And here, where dykes now drain the marshy land
Away from ocean, where the ancient sand
Is thinly cover'd with a porous soil,
Which scarce rewards the working peasant's toil,

Whilst digging sandy earth maybe his spade
An anchor finds—in Roman days 'twas made.
Hope's rusty emblem centuries buried lay,
And resting still till now this Christian day.
O'er marshland frown'd a Roman stately camp,
Whose ancient fort now marks the well-known stamp
Of cultivation rife—of Raleigh's import rare—
Industrious coastguard's leisure hour and care,
As pipe in mouth from erst his duty free,
When hoeing ground he then has chanc'd to see
A rounded outline 'mongst the upturn'd mould,
Which cleans'd reveals a laurell'd Cæsar bold ;[4]
Reverse is seen she-wolf's illustrious brood.
Such coins now found intact for many a rood,
'Hap 'tis Constantius who to Britain sent
Lup'cinus, who then had reach'd to Kent,[5]
Or Emp'ror Claudius who had sent his hosts
To stay pirates from ravaging our coasts,
Or Theodosius of Roman fame.
Reward the senate then did well ordain,
That noble deeds by him should e'er be known
By marble statue fix'd full high at Rome.
Such laurell'd heroes' chisell'd features fine
Come forth on coins from out the womb of time.

The summer-folk from round the neighb'ring bay
Stroll 'midst these ruins—make the place their stay
At pleasure's call—but the reflective mind
Will here grave food for close reflection find,
In greatness vast that flow'd from Tiber's strand,
That conquer'd ours with bearded warlike band,
And back again the land from whence they came,
Came down from conqu'ror, and but left a name.
From rev'ries' thoughts on all the bygone age,
Lo! where the coastguard goes by easy stage,
On duty bent his well-worn walk to pace.
Old sailors love their bygones still to trace,
Advent'rous scenes where now in sunny lands
The waving palms grow down to golden sands;
Where coral-reefs surround their desert isles,
And thousands more extend for many miles;
How in the tropics' hot and weary days
Becalm'd they lay in placid lukewarm waves,
Or northward voyage when they whaling go
To lands of ice-blinks and eternal snow;
Here Esquimaux in snow-built hut is found,
From wintry blasts shut up, that chill the ground,
The elements defying—eats his winter store,
Sleeps off his time, and wants but little more.

When summer suns again shine on through snow,
To haunts of walrus he prepares to go
With sledge in order, sharpens all his spears,
And for the ice-bound north he gladly steers
His half-fed dogs, with whip-thong's lash to smack
And dash along—he makes the old ice crack.
On whaling trip how many whales they struck,
And many tons of oil fell to their luck ;
With well-fill'd hatches gain'd the open sea,
With fair wind's help soon reach'd grand old Dundee.
Contentment reigns full oft in sailor's mind,
In him philosophy we often find.
From years of sailing well the billows' foam,
On Albion's cliffs he finds his life and home.
When o'er Reculvers' rock rough winds still roar,
The coastguard stands at duty on the shore ;
Aloft the sea-bird's note sounds o'er the waste,
Re-echoing still—her nest she seeks in haste.
Reculvers made, my wand'ring steps I shape,
And now the breezy upland path I take,
Where meadow-sweet spreads o'er the verdant plains,
'Twixt hedges bound with fragrant woodbine chains,
Past cottage, bright with summer and with flowers,
Where butterflies yet frisk their sunny hours ;

Where Canterbury-bells and picotees,
And bordered marigolds, and gay heartsease,
Larkspur and lupin, and bright flowers that vie
In finding sweets for bees, which hum close by.

FORD PALACE.[6]

Where shady lanes lead down to Ford's still dell,
Those priestly builders show they knew full well

OLD WALL OF THE PALACE OF FORD, WITH LEAN-TO SHEDS.

How shelter make from cold, rude Boreas' blast,
Which winter here oft sends, and furious fast.
Old crumbling walls by hoary time are scor'd,
And tottering ruins mark the site of Ford,

Relics of where a stately Palace stood,

Whose ancient front had cover'd many a rood.

'Twas here the great Reformer Cranmer sought

The rest he richly earn'd at Henry's Court.

These mossy walls, with Roman brick inlaid,

Are fraught with mem'ries vast that never fade ;

The kitchen, relic left of ancient pile,

Survives in use with florid floor of tile ;

Here many a cautious carp has made a fry,

Caught from the pond in garden still close by.

A holy calm now reigns the Palace round,

Quiescence e'er the mark of saintly ground,

Save buzz of bees beneath the southern wall,

Where cluster'd ripening fruits are fain to fall—

Apricot, nect'rine, rosy peach, and pear,

The purple plum and sweet greengage, are there.

From shelter'd farm there come the country sounds,

Which break the stillness that pervades the grounds,

As kine now lowing in their old thatch'd shed,

And pigeons cooing, nestling overhead,

Or pleasant jingling of the milkmaid's pail,

As milking now she goes adown the dale.

Where sun's soft rays in summer always fall,

And ripen grapes, which cluster ancient wall ;

The crannied nook, which rears the creeping plant,
The tiny insect, and oft busy ant ;
And shines on flies, that skimming o'er the flowers,
The colour'd beauties of a few brief hours,
With hum of insects make a harmony,
And varied birds that warble melody.

FORD.

Reclining on a time-worn garden seat,
In leafy shade, out of the summer's heat,
Above the scented honeysuckle twines,
And overhead the tangled jess'mine binds ;
Where water-lilies swim lake's rippling breast,
'Mongst these old garden flowers 'tis sweet to rest,

In gardens fraught with mem'ries of the past;
Of days when martyr'd Cranmer at the last,
Hail'd life immortal for the holy cause,
And fell to harsh Queen Mary's bigot laws.

HAW FARM.

At Ford refresh'd, I ramble on again,
Where clust'ring hop clothes all the fertile plain,

HOP GARDENS.

And climbing steeps, to where there stands afar
A thick wood, shelt'ring now the farm of Haw.

HOP-PICKING.

To hearts how many does this fond sound mean
A spell of rural days in golden green

Of Kentish lanes, where wand'ring pickers roam,
And barns and leafy hedgerows form their home.
When autumn sun has pal'd the rip'ning hop,
Here clust'ring poles, there waving o'er the top,
Call pickers young and old to sport with glee.
Engaging fun to them—all bright and free
From smoke and noise, far from the busy town,
With pale, wan faces now become so brown—
To chase the flies that paint the wayside flowers,
And seek the shelter of the hawthorn's bowers,
To list to birds, which when the rain is o'er,
'Mong glist'ning leaves their sweetest songs outpour.
The gardens reach'd, the serious work begins.
Whilst willing hands now soon the hop-bine thins,
To hop-oasts great, hard by the neighb'ring hill,
Are taken baskets they unceasing fill.
The gardens finish'd, homeward wend their way,
And thank the hops for glorious holiday.

HAW FARM—*continued.*

The buildings here are all of ancient date,[7]
With Gothic windows in a crumbling state,

And Tudor chimneys, and strong buttress'd walls,
And fish-ponds round for fast-days—fancy palls
To lift her airy wings and roam around
The cinctur'd portals of this ancient ground.
The ruddy brick now mould'ring with decay,
From which the mortar falls so fast away,

HAW FARM.

Where Tudor lozenge, in a darker brick,
Bestrews these walls, constructed hard and thick,
And still on ancient grange is often seen.
Maybe a grange this old farmhouse has been.

THE ANCIENT GRANGE.[8]

What charm at leisure freely far to range
In nooks and corners of some moated grange,
Where o'er the ancient porch we faintly trace
The mould'ring 'scutcheon of some lordly race,
Or mottoed crest they all so bravely bore
In holy wars so fierce, in battles yore,
High on their helmets in the thick of fight,
Or work'd in gold on pond'rous shields so bright,
Which flash'd in sunshine o'er proud Asc'lon's plain,
'Mid Eastern spears which fell as thick as rain.
In hall where hangs the mail of Norman lord,
His gauntlets, lance, and strong two-handed sword,
'Mong ancient weapons, trophies of the chase,
Are wheel-lock pistols, and cross-bow, and mace.
The grim old portraits hanging round the wall,
Those dim old heroes of far days recall,
Of warriors brave still marking Tudor times,
Who found their graves in far-off foreign climes.
Some who, when mighty Spain's Armada sought
These shores—experience so dearly bought,
To fight in battle like the Vikings old,
Whose valiant deeds are still in story told,

Proud Spain to shake and bring her to the dust.
Our nations gain on sea—all else to thrust.

HAW FARM—*continued.*

From fancy's call to real Haw's old courts,
Suggesting still quaint antiquarian thoughts ;
No weapon here, or trophy hangs of chase,
Nor ancient portraits is there any trace ;
Not even flow'rets gay cheer passers by,
The Kentish scene alone now charms the eye.
A weird and leafless tree in lonely state,
An emblem of the sad decree of fate,
Harmonious with its old dismantled charm,
To add a tribute still to old Haw Farm.

HERNE VILLAGE.9

From Haw we pass a windmill on the right,
Through ev'ning mist, and Herne is near to sight,
Its church towers gilt—the sun on gorgeous throne,
On cluster'd hamlet lurid rays had shone ;
The village smoke now melts with purple haze,
Its lattice panes reflect Sol's flick'ring blaze,

Enwraps the village and the old church tower,
And like the parish clock proclaims the hour
When evening meal now cheers the eventide,
And tired lab'rers seek their snug fireside.
St. Martin's bells now chime the fleeting hour.
Here martyr'd Ridley some time held the cure ;

HERNE VILLAGE AND CHURCH.

Through time-worn porch a-down the ancient nave
Has Ridley walk'd with stately step and grave,
From pulpit quaint would eloquently flow
Those stirring words, that told how sure, if slow,
Was marching Reformation near at hand
To crush the Popish power throughout our land,

To show how sure the brave Reformer spread

His doctrine true when darkness reign'd ; to shed

The light which superstition held in mist,

Which ages long before had still exist.

Our stolid ignorance was trodden o'er

With priestly pomp—by deferential power.

The sermon o'er, the blessing, calm and meek,

With fervour giv'n, gently he then would seek

The trees' deep shade—there talk on church affairs

With gray-hair'd folk, all bent with life-long cares ;

Or linger by the old church wicket gate,

To mildly censure boys, who chance came late ;

That gate where schoolboys on warm summer days

Amuse themselves in various schoolboy ways,

Or scan their lessons learnt the night before,

But scarce prepar'd when opes the school-house door.

The dial causes sad and wistful looks

As eyes are taken off their dog-ear'd books.

That clock-tower's walls, though weather-worn, still show

The quarter whence the wintry winds now blow,

Whose shadow hides the well-worn mossy mounds,

In peace to wait the last trump's wak'ning sounds.

A fond and tender love maternal shines,

Sad epitaph is here in touching lines :

" A little spirit slumbers here,

   Who to one heart was very dear.

   Oh ! he was more than light or life ;

   Its thought by day, its dream by night.

HERNE STREET, WITH ENTRANCE TO CHURCHYARD.

The chill winds came, the young flower fades,

And died—the grave its sweetness hides.

Fair boy, thou should'st have wept for me,

Not I have had to mourn o'er thee.

Yet not long shall this sorrowing be ;

The roses I have planted round,

To deck thy dear, sad, sacred ground,

When next spring gales these roses wave,

They'll blossom o'er thy mother's grave."

Here quietly at rest in mournful state,

Should each narrate his grim and ancient fate.

The village annals would they then unfold,

And many tales of other days be told :

How Ridley from his ancient pulpit spoke,

And boldly preach'd 'gainst bigot Queen and Pope ;

When persecuted did not conscience turn,

With holy martyrs at the stake did burn ;

And would then still relate, how awe-struck group

Around their village church with grief would stoop

To offer prayers for pastor of their days,

Then each go on and turn their sev'ral ways.

This trouble in those days was sorely rife,

Each village had its element of strife ;

Of captious folk each neighbour was afraid,

Nor dar'd for very life to church have stray'd ;

An " Ave " or his beads alone to tell
At sound of "matins" or the "vesper" bell.
Mayhap the church bells for this service rung,
Or silent were when Latin prayers were sung,
In belfry high, in firm yet mute disdain,
They waited better times to come again.

The Village Bells.

When o'er remote and distant lands we roam,
Our thoughts oft turn towards our far-off home ;
A herd's deep lowing, or the tinkling bell
Where flocking sheep are feeding o'er the fell,
Or village chimes may greet the list'ning ear
Like those oft heard when love and home are near !
These simple sounds may waken in our breast
A train of thought that's long since gone to rest.
So when return'd, his service-time expir'd,
A soldier home to live his days retir'd.
Worn, weary, seeking then his native vale,
He hears from far, borne on the summer gale,
The bells, sweet sound to him—their sound flows on,
Now swelling with the wind, now nearly gone ;
The fresh'ning breeze now bears them nearer still,
As wearied out he mounts the toilsome hill ;

The summit reach'd, his village lay below,
Old thoughts return and make his bosom glow
With love for those he hopes to see once more,
His waking thoughts when on the distant shore.
Oft when at break of day by bugle's call
From home-dreams summon'd in his ranks to fall,
And march o'er deserts where the scorching ray
Of tropic's sun there quivers all the day,
O'er trackless wastes to where the Arab band,
" Allah ! " on lips, now charge across the sand,
Wave holy banners o'er their desert paths
And desolation bring to many hearths,
His village scarce thought he to see again,
Or hear its chimes still wafted o'er the plain ;
So now these bells, borne on the summer gale,
Seem ringing welcome to his native vale.

HERNE VILLAGE—*continued.*

The church's panes so storied prisms show,
In varied tints the letter'd pavements glow
On ancient brass, which cut by cunning hand,
To where the screens in fretted arches stand,
On mural tablets where is faintly read
The Latin glories of the ancient dead.

"Te Deum" here was first in English sung,
Long years its chant was in the Latin tongue.
Old churches, these mementoes of the past,
O'er village life true sentiment have cast.
They stand now where as in the darker age,
Before the sound translation of that page,
Enabling England's sons themselves to read
That book on which they found their native creed ;
And ere the prayer-book's true religious form,
Which since Sixth Edward's time, on Sabbath morn,
We render thanks for all His mercies giv'n,
Health, calm contentment, hop'd-for rest in heaven.

CONTENTMENT.

Contentment sweet, what comfort in the sound,
Where life is bliss and joys diffus'd around ;
Time was when poets wrote sweet roundelays
For shepherds and their nymphs to sing thy praise,
In sylvan groves beneath the leafy shade,
With oaken branches stretching o'er the glade,
Whilst minding sheep with shepherds' ribbon'd crooks.
These shepherds now are only found in books,
Where Wheatley's pencil decorates the page,
Old-fashioned taste—yet now the bookworm's rage ;

Or Wattcau's beauties 'midst the sylvan throng
To piping shepherds dance the hours along.
Still sweet contentment is quite free to all,
If on its aids we are dispos'd to call.
Who village-born still dwells in rural cot,
His thoughts all centred round this much-lov'd spot ;

HERNE VILLAGE.

His frugal wants by rustic labour found,
Each month brings work to tillers of the ground.
With prompt departure at the break of day,
When sun o'er casement sends his wak'ning ray,

He starts for work, and hails the rosy morn
With grateful thanks for balmy spring-days born.
His careful wife the morning meal prepares,
Which o'er, is busied with her household cares.
The elder children to the school are sent,
Whilst younger ones sit in the porch, content
In sunny hours to play near mother's eye.
Their rosy cheeks oft charm the passer-by ;
When old enough, by careful parent shown
To give Him thanks for all they are and own,
Before each meal repeat the humble prayer,
And lisp the grace for good and homely fare.
A godly life with cleanliness is found,
Their cot more neat than all the village round ;
The garden front, the goodman's ev'ning care,
The flowers each season brings are planted there.
O'er trellis'd porch the tendrils slender seek,
Clematis fair and cultur'd woodbine meek ;
His garden patch his labour well repays,
There oft he spends his well-earn'd holidays.
Religious doubts not here disturb his breast,
The creed he first learnt still he thinks the best ;
In rural quiet together pass through life,
Content to share its cares and soothe its strife.

HERNE VILLAGE—*continued.*

In other spots, as in this tranquil Herne,
Such homes and cots we fairly may discern ;
The forge is there, where youth on errands stay,
To watch at eve its beam to cross the way ;
The useful shop, where, when the matrons meet,
The latest gossip oft their tongues repeat ;
The inn's snug parlour, where the lab'rers pass
Long winter's nights, with song and social glass,
Where farmers meet to talk about their crops,
Discuss the weather, and report on hops.
The length'ning day drags slow towards melting eve,
Herne's nestling village with regret I leave,
Down dusty road, and homewards make my way.
Sun o'er the landscape sends th' expiring ray,
The summer cloud reflects the yellow gold,
The careful shepherd calls the scatter'd fold ;
Tir'd harvesters return bronz'd with the sun,
Some riding in the wain—their day's work done.
The geese all dimly seen in gloam beyond
To settle there beside the sedgy pond.
O'er hillside now is heard a cheerful horn,
And noise of wheels and prancing steeds—'tis gone.

The Canterbury coach[9] pass'd on its way,
On journey home to Herne's wide bracing bay.
A charming trip 'tis when the weather's fine,
And ev'ning ride winds up the passing time;
Where old cathedral's towers now pierce the sky,
Whilst ancient glories still enchant the eye.

THE "LITTLE WONDER" COACH PASSING THROUGH EDDINGTON.

HERNE BAY.[10]

The bracing sea-breeze blows fresh in my face
As nearing now this thriving seaside place,
With long parade, and cleanly asphalte paths,
Its fresh'ning air and pleasant saline baths,

Pavilion, walks which lead to pier and band,

Green shelving cliffs and far out-stretching sand;

Home comforts here are not for me to tell,

On rural charms I always long'd to dwell.

I fear my pen but fails when it describes

The beauty of the neighb'ring walks and drives.

Here Nature is display'd in all her hues:

Streams, woods, and cornfields, and far-distant views.

When from the Blean the visual rays are sent,

See fruitful vales of charming " Weald of Kent."

Look east where Phœbus rides in roseate car,

Lo there—cropp'd Thanet's isle you see from far.

Look west where Father Thames in all his pride,

With Medway join'd, there rolls a mighty tide.[11]

I now leave other pens inclin'd to tell

Of healthy walks, and beauties known so well;

But on this breezy coast, with those lov'd best,

And sharing simple pleasures, seeking rest,

Sweet 'tis to ramble out on summer day,

'Mid rural scenes that charm at bright Herne Bay.

　　　　　　　　S. THEOBALD SMITH.

NOTES.

[1] St. Augustine was sent by Pope Gregory I., in the year A.D. 596, to convert the inhabitants of Britain to Christianity. Ethelbert, King of Kent, and head of the Heptarchy, having married a Christian princess, daughter of Charibert, King of Paris, and niece to Chilperic, favoured the chances of the mission being received, which ultimately proved to be the case ; as on Ethelbert hearing the saint and his followers had landed at Ebbsfleet, he, accompanied by Queen Bertha, went to Thanet, and received them in the open air. The Venerable Bede gives the words of the King, on hearing St. Augustine describe the object of his mission. " Your proposals are noble," said the king, " and your promises inviting ; yet I cannot resolve upon quitting the religion of my ancestors for one that appears to me supported only by the testimony of persons who are entire strangers to me. Since, however, as I perceive that you have undertaken so long a journey on purpose to impart to us those things which you deem most important and valuable, you shall not be sent away without some satisfaction. I will take care that you shall be treated with civility, and supplied with all things necessary and convenient ; and if any of my people, convinced by your arguments, desire to embrace your faith, I will not oppose it." Bede, who is the authority for most of the historical and ecclesiastical accounts of this period, was born in 672 ; and as St. Augustine died in 619, about eighty years would elapse. In this interval the monks, no

44   *NOTES.*

doubt, had carefully noted down what occurred at so interesting a period in their history. Bede died in 735. King Ethelbert, partly through his own convictions, and partly owing to the persuasions of Queen Bertha, was, with many of his subjects, converted to Christianity, relinquishing his palace at Canterbury to St. Augustine, and, retiring to his palace at Reculvers, ultimately died there.

² As, beside the few Roman walls, the church forms the only remains of the once important Reculvers, I will therefore briefly quote from writers who viewed this church at various periods, to give some idea of the objects of interest that these now bare walls once contained. John Leland, writing at the time of Henry VIII., describing this church, says : "At the entrance to the choir was one of the fairest and most stately crosses that he ever saw ; it was some feet in height, and stood like a fair column. The second stone was round, and had images of Christ and some of His Apostles, curiously wrought, with labels from their mouths painted in large Roman letters. The next stone exhibited the Passion of our Saviour. The next above that had the twelve Apostles. The fifth had our Saviour nailed to the cross, with a sustentaculem under His feet ; and the uppermost stone was in the form of a cross. He also saw an ancient book of the Gospels, in large Roman letters, and in the boards thereof a chrystal stone inscribed, 'Claudia Alcpiccus'; also a painted figure of a bishop under an arch." Weever, writing later, says : "At the upper end of the south aisle he saw a monument of an antique form, mounted with two spires, in which, as tradition reports, lay the body of King Ethelbert I., the fifth King of Kent, and first Christian monarch." The Rev. J. Pridden, writing in 1781, describes several monuments and brasses as being then in the church, notably Sir Cavaliero Maycote's, with figures of himself, wife and nine children, with crest and arms ; also Ralph Brook's and Sandeway's. Ralph Brook was York Herald at the period of James I. ; he lived in a house near Reculvers of which only the gateway is now standing.

In 1809, after Reculvers Church had ceased to be used as a place of worship, the parishioners, supposing it was left a prey to the sea, dismantled it, and took the lead off the roof ; and doubtless it would have entirely disappeared, but for the intervention of the Directors of the Trinity House, who preserved it for the purposes of navigation.

³ This stream, which is now but a few feet across, was once an important channel, entirely separating Thanet from the mainland, defended by two important Roman forts, the Castle of Regulbium at Reculvers, and the Castle of Rutupium at Richborough. Harold steered his fleet through this strait when he sailed from Sandwich to London. The monks of St. Augustine, in the year 1313, claimed all wrecks in their manor of Menstre (Minster), Chistelet, and Stodmersch. There was a naval station at Saar, midway between Richborough and Reculvers. According to John Twine, who died in 1581, in his time "eight credible men were living who affirmed that they had seen not only small boats, but large loaded vessels, frequently pass and re-pass between the island (Isle of Thanet) and the continent (Britain)."

⁴ An authority states: "Coins have been found here occasionally for many years, and are mostly Roman, the heads being either crowned with laurel or diadem ; on the reverse, military engines, horsemen overthrowing an enemy, or the she-wolf with Romulus and Remus."

⁵ Camden says : "Lupicinus, sent by Constantius into Britain to check the inroads of the Scots and Picts, landed here (Reculvers) his companies of the Heruli, Batavi, and Moesici. Theodosius also, father of the Emperor of that name, to whom, according to Symmachus, the Senate voted equestrian statues for restoring tranquillity to Britain, came hither with his Herculean, Jovian, Victorius, and Fidentine cohorts. Afterwards, when the Saxon pirates put a stop to commerce, made the sea a scene of war, and infested our coasts with their continual ravages, the Legio II. Augusta, which the Emperor Claudius had brought out of

Germany, and which had been fixed many years at Isca Silurum, in Wales, was removed hither, and had its officer here under the Count of the Saxon shore."

6 The ancient Palace of Ford stood partly in the parish of Hoath and partly in that of Chislet. A few crumbling walls, and what is now called the " monks' kitchen," is all that remains of one of the most ancient of the archiepiscopal palaces belonging to the see of Canterbury, having been given to it by King Ethelbert. Archbishop Cranmer resided much at Ford ; he was here at the time the Plague was at Lambeth, 1537, when the Bible was first published in English. He also reviewed the "Articles of Religion" here in 1552 ; and it is stated that, suffering from ague at Croydon in that summer, he removed to Ford in October. Archbishop Parker would have pulled the Palace down, but for the opposition he met with from the Queen. It was afterwards demolished by order of the Commonwealth, 1658, and the bricks and timber sold.

7 The buildings on this farm have a decided ecclesiastical character ; the walls are of great thickness, and are pierced with Gothic windows at regular intervals, which give it every appearance of having at one time been used as a monastic establishment or convent ; also the range of ponds, and the sheltered position of the whole, suggest a site that would be chosen for a religious house. Haw forms one of the five boroughs of the parish of Herne.

8 This digression was suggested in this way : whilst sketching in the neighbourhood of Haw Farm, and being overtaken by the shades of evening, on passing that side of the old farmhouse where the pond washes the foundations, the surroundings being shrouded in gloom, the effect was precisely as though the water surrounded the buildings as in old moated houses. With regard to the description of the interior, although I admit there is nothing of the kind here, yet it may not be considered out of place in a Kentish Garland, the description answering to that of other houses in a

county noted for its hops, pretty faces, and grand old historic mansions.

⁹ Herne is a good specimen, in its primitive state, of one of those old English villages with which the county of Kent is so rich. Most of its houses would date back several centuries, and with its fine old church, it offers a pleasing view from whatever point it is seen. The church, which is dedicated to St. Martin, contains many monuments and objects of interest, and is rendered historically interesting from the fact of Bishop Ridley having in his early days been collated to the vicarage by Cranmer. "Here he was diligent to instruct his charge in the pure doctrines of the Gospel as far as they were yet discovered to him (not from the schoolmen and popish doctors), except in the point of transubstantiation, from which error God had not yet delivered him." Ridley spent a great part of the year 1545 in retirement at Herne, and probably carrying with him an Apology, published by the Zwinglians for their exploding the doctrine of transubstantiation, he gave the question a fair examination, and discovered its sophistry. Archbishop Cranmer and Bishop Latimer were both convinced of the fallacy of this doctrine through the investigations of Bishop Ridley. In 1547 Ridley was presented with the vicarage of Soham, Cambridgeshire, and, the September following, to the see of Rochester, from thence raised to the see of London, 1550. In his last farewell, when under sentence of death, to all the places with which he had been in any way connected, Herne is thus distinguished : "From Cambridge I was called into Kent by the Archbishop of Canterbury, Thomas Cranmer, that most reverend father and man of God, and of him by-and-by sent to be vicar of Herne, in East Kent. Wherefore, farewell, Herne, thou worshipful and wealthy parish ! the first cure whereunto I was called to minister God's word. Thou hast heard of my mouth ofttimes the word of God preached, not after the Popish trade, but after Christ's Gospel. Oh that the fruit had answered to the seed ! And yet I must acknowledge me to be

thy debtor for the doctrine of the Lord's Supper, which at that time God had not revealed to me." Bishop Ridley, with Bishop Latimer, suffered martyrdom at Oxford, 1555.

[10] Those who might wish for more information about this very pleasant seaside resort, I can refer to an excellent book on Herne Bay and neighbourhood, entitled " Herne Bay Illustrated."

[11] Gray, the poet, writing to a friend, thus describes this part of Kent: " I was surprised at the beauty of the road round Canterbury. The whole country is a rich cultivated garden ; orchards, cherry grounds, hop plantations, intermixed with corn-fields and villages, gentle risings covered with trees, and in the distance the Thames and the Medway breaking on the landscape, with all their navigation." As this is the only part of the country near Canterbury where views of the Thames and Medway can together be obtained, we may fairly assume that it was in driving out in this direction that the poet passed through the scenery about which he wrote in such glowing terms to his friend.

THE END.

CHARLES DICKENS AND EVANS, CRYSTAL PALACE PRESS.